Jesus Is God's Son

BOOK 6 OF TOGETHER: A DISCIPLESHIP SERIES FOR PARENT AND CHILD

By Linda Corbin & Pat Dys

CHRISTIAN PUBLICATIONS

Camp Hill, Pennsylvania

Contents

✝ The mark of vibrant faith

Christian Publications

Publishing House of The Christian and Missionary Alliance

3825 Hartzdale Drive, Camp Hill, PA 17011

© 1988 by Christian Publications. All rights reserved

ISBN:0-87509-404-X

Printed in the United States of America

Unless otherwise indicated, all Scripture quotations are taken from the HOLY BIBLE: NEW INTERNATIONAL VERSION. Copyright © 1973, 1978, 1984 by the International Bible Society. Used by permission of Zondervan Bible Publishers.

Preface

The church today is catching the vision of discipleship. With renewed zeal, believers are developing close relationships with new converts, spending time with them studying God's Word on a one-to-one basis. The results are encouraging.

In our fervor to disciple new converts, however, we have often neglected a systematic, organized discipleship of our own children. They too are included in our job description found in Colossians 1:28–29: "So everywhere we go we talk about Christ to all who will listen, warning them and teaching them as well as we know how. We want to be able to present each one to God, perfect because of what Christ has done for each of them. This is my work, and I can do it only because Christ's mighty energy is at work within me" (TLB).

As parents and church leaders, we gradually realized that most of our energies were spent on plans, programs and pursuits involving church ministries, while the discipling of our own children was occurring happenstance. Certainly we were faithful in family devotions and Scripture memory with the children, but we had no long-range spiritual growth program.

To find such a program, we searched the Christian literature market and discovered that no parent-child discipleship book existed. So, we set out to develop our own. As others expressed enthusiasm and interest in it, this discipleship series developed.

Written for children ages 6–11, *Jesus Is God's Son* can be narrowed to simple levels for the young child and broadened into more complex discoveries for the older child. The Scripture provided in each lesson is by no means exhaustive on that particular subject. If at any time your child shows a continued interest in the subject, be sure to study additional relevant passages together.

The *Together* workbook series is designed to be used with your child on a one-to-one basis. It is not intended for family devotions. Children thrive on individualized attention from their parents, and what better way to spend that time than to teach spiritual truths?

Do one lesson a week with your child. We have found that bedtime is a good share-time, because children are generally more eager to talk then. Since little preparation is needed, simply read through the lesson, discuss the Scriptures and answer the questions. The lesson itself will take 20–30 minutes, depending upon the interest and ability of your child. As you progress, however, we encourage you to remind your child of what you learned together, so he will learn to incorporate it into his life.

As you begin this adventure together, remember that true discipleship is pouring your life into the life of another. Let your child know that this time alone with him or her is special. Learn the Bible verses together and quiz each other. Become involved with weekly assignments. Share yourself—your spiritual victories *and* defeats. As your child recognizes Jesus to be real in your life, you will see that same Jesus becoming real in his or her life.

Happy discipling!

Linda Corbin and Pat Dys

How to Use the Together Series

If you are using the *Together* series for the first time, we recommend that you begin with the first five books in the series: *Jesus Makes Us New*, *Jesus Helps Me Grow*, *Jesus Lights the Way*, *Jesus Teaches Me* and *Jesus Wants Us to Obey*. It is important that your child has the proper spiritual foundation before you continue with Book 6, *Jesus Is God's Son*.

Each lesson is divided between information for the parent and for the child. The parent's information is always on the left-hand side of the page in the shaded column. This section includes the aim of the lesson along with hints, thoughts and reminders that will help you teach the lesson at a glance. Each suggestion is directly opposite its corresponding section of the child's lesson.

If studying the Bible is new to you, Background Notes are provided at the bottom of the parent's column. These are not exhaustive, but they will help you with any questions your child may ask. Be sure to read this section prior to the discipleship lesson.

The child's column, on the right-hand side of every page, contains some or all of the following lesson material:

THINK AGAIN This section includes one or two brief suggestions to help you review the previous lesson. Children enjoy repetition and need this overview in order to build each lesson on the last and successfully grasp this Christian growth series.

IDEA WORD In every lesson, one or two words provide the main idea for that session. The words are usually concepts that require discussion in order for the child to grasp them. You can begin your discussion with the Idea Word and allow the rest of the lesson to help define the meaning of the concept.

READ AND REMEMBER A Scripture verse is listed here along with the text. You may read it directly from the workbook or ask your child to read it from his or her own Bible. All Scripture

throughout the workbook is taken from the New International Version of the Bible. This same verse also appears in the Hands On section as the memory verse of the week. Encourage your child to print the text on an index card and tape it to a bedroom mirror or desk so it is constantly in view.

If Scripture memory is new to you and your child, we encourage you to actively participate in it. Frequent repetition of both the verse and its reference is necessary for full mastery.

Break the verse into several word phrases and concentrate on mastering each phrase until you can put them all together. Another helpful method is to write the verse on a chalkboard or marker board and read it together. Then begin erasing one word at a time, adding the words from memory. You will no doubt be amazed at how your child can learn even more readily than you!

DO YOU KNOW? A paragraph and set of questions is provided that begins to define the Idea Word of the lesson. A Bible story that illustrates the Idea Word is also given to help the child understand God's Word more fully. You may elaborate further on the child's level once you have laid the groundwork.

FIND OUT Encourage your child to use his or her own Bible to answer these questions. You might even want to write in the answers to the questions in the white spaces on the page.

TALK TO GOD These brief suggestions for prayer time can be used as parent and child pray together.

HANDS ON This activity section augments the learning process by providing application ideas for the lesson. The memory verse of the week is included here as a reminder to memorize it for the coming lesson.

We Worship One God

CHILD

AIM:
To help your child develop a basic understanding of what the Trinity is: three in one.

Note: *3 in 1 (A Picture of God)* by Joanne Marxhausen, © 1973, Concordia, is an excellent presentation of the Trinity for a young child.

THOUGHTS:
The Trinity is difficult for a child to comprehend. Some other illustrations might help explain the concept. An egg has three parts — shell, yolk, white — yet it is one egg. An ear of corn has three parts — kernel, cob, husk — yet it is one ear.

IDEA WORD: Trinity

READ AND REMEMBER:

John 15:26 — "When the Counselor comes, whom I will send to you from the Father, the Spirit of truth who goes out from the Father, he will testify about me."

DO YOU KNOW?

The Bible tells us that there is only one God to worship. He made us. He loves us. He wants us to live with Him forever. And He shows Himself to us in three different ways: as God the Father, Jesus Christ the Son and the Holy Spirit. We call this the *Trinity* or the three Persons that make up one God.

How can one thing be three? Well think about water. Water has three different forms. It can be an ice cube or a glass of water or the steam from a boiling pan of water. No matter what form you have, each one is still water. Just as each part of God is still God.

Read Deuteronomy 6:1–9 where God tells the

5

Israelites that He is their only God, and they are to love and worship Him.

HINTS:
Emphasize that we worship only *one* God. In fact, to have more than one God is idolatry and condemned in the Bible (Exodus 20:3–5a).

As you read the different ministries of each member of the Trinity, note that God sent Jesus because of His love for man. One of Jesus' primary tasks was leading people to God. See Background Note 1 for further discussion on Luke 19:10, John 6:38 and 14:6.

Discuss the ministry of the Holy Spirit in our lives today. See Background Note 2 for help.

FIND OUT:

★ How many Gods are there? Read Deuteronomy 6:4.

★ Although there is only one God, He shows Himself as three different Persons and each Person has a different job. Read these verses to see what God the Father has done for us: John 3:16 and 6:44.

★ What is the job of God the Son, Jesus? The answer can be found in Luke 19:10, John 6:38 and 14:6.

★ What work does the Holy Spirit do? Read John 16:7–8, 13–14 for the answer.

BACKGROUND NOTES:
1. The work of God the Son is to bring people to God:
Luke 19:10—Jesus' whole purpose in coming was to seek and to save the lost. He had an answer for people in sin.
John 6:38—God sent Jesus to earth, not to do as He pleased, but to do what the Father wanted Him to do. He had a specific mission to accomplish: to lead people to God.
John 14:6—Jesus is the only way, the only truth and the only life. Apart from Him we cannot reach God.
2. God the Spirit (Holy Spirit) works in the lives of people. In John 16 He is described as a Counselor because He comes to advise the believer; as a Convictor because He shows men their sin; as a Guide because He teaches the believer in all truth; and as a Glorifier because He brings glory and honor to Jesus rather than to Himself.

TALK TO GOD:

God has given us Himself as Father, Son and Holy Spirit. In this way He is able to meet every need we have. Thank Him for always being there when you need Him.

HANDS ON:

This week take time to praise God for each Person in the Trinity. Try to think of at least one thing that God the Father, Jesus and the Holy Spirit have done for you.

Memorize John 15:26—"When the Counselor comes, whom I will send to you from the Father, the Spirit of truth who goes out from the Father, he will testify about me."

The One and Only God

CHILD

THINK AGAIN:

Did you thank God for the Trinity last week? Share some things that God the Father, Jesus the Son and the Holy Spirit have done for you. If you forgot, go back to the Find Out section in Lesson 1 for the answers.

IDEA WORD: One God

READ AND REMEMBER:

Psalm 86:10 — "For you are great and do marvelous deeds; you alone are God."

DO YOU KNOW?

There is only one God in the whole world. There are many mothers, fathers, children and teachers, but there is only one God. And that one God who made the whole world — the trees, the animals, the moun-

tains, the oceans, the sky and every person — knows and loves you! If you turn to Deuteronomy 4:32–40, you will find some more wonderful things that God has done. God tells us these things so we will know that He is the one and only God.

HINTS:
Discuss the first commandment in the context of Exodus 20:1–6. See Background Note 1 for further explanation.

After reading the memory verse, note that He is more than the only God — He is also great and does great works.

Following Hezekiah's example, stress the need for praising God. Since He is so great, we must tell Him so.

Tell the story of Naaman from 2 Kings 5:1–15. See Background Note 2 for a brief summary.

Help your child understand what an idol is. Discuss God versus idols using Background Note 3.

FIND OUT:

★ Turn to Exodus 20:3. What was the first commandment God gave to His people?

★ Turn again to Psalm 86:10. What does the Bible tell us about this one and only God?

★ What did Hezekiah say when he prayed to God? Read 2 Kings 19:15.

★ After God healed Naaman of leprosy, what was Naaman's response? Find the answer in 2 Kings 5:15.

★ Not everybody believes in one God. Some people pray to many gods. Read Psalm 115:2–9 to find out how God is different from these other gods.

BACKGROUND NOTES:
1. When God gave Moses the Ten Commandments, the very first one read: "You shall have no other gods before me." As we note the context, we can see the reason for this. Jehovah God Himself, alone, had freed the Israelites from Egyptian captivity. He had protected them and provided for them in their 40 years of wandering in the wilderness. He alone was able to continue providing for them. And, their part was to honor Him as their only God for that is just what He was and is.
2. God healed Naaman of leprosy:
a. Naaman was an excellent army commander of the King of Aram.
b. But he had leprosy, a contagious, incurable disease.
c. A captive Israelite girl was a servant to Naaman's wife.
d. She told her mistress that a prophet (Elisha) could heal Naaman.
e. Namaan went to him and was told to bathe in the Jordan River seven times.
f. When he did so, he was cleansed of leprosy.
g. His response was to acknowledge Israel's one God.
3. An idol is something people worship instead of God. In many countries people make little statues and pray to them, or they pray to rocks or sticks. The psalmist says, though, that they cannot see, hear, speak, smell, feel or walk.

We too can sometimes have idols. They may not be carved statues, but they are things we value more than God and look to when we have trouble: friends, money, possessions, horoscopes, etc.

TALK TO GOD:

Remember King Hezekiah's prayer of praise in 2 Kings 19:15? You too need to tell God how wonderful He is.

HANDS ON:

This week, take time every day to tell God how wonderful He is. Start making a list of all the things God has done for you, then it will not be at all hard to praise Him. To make this easier, pick a certain time of day to read your list and praise God. Maybe the best time would be in the morning when you see the bright blue sky and shiny yellow sun. Or maybe the best time for you would be in the evening when you see millions of stars in the sky and wonder how God made them all.

Memorize Psalm 86:10 — "For you are great and do marvelous deeds; you alone are God."

Before the Beginning

CHILD

THINK AGAIN:

Did you remember to praise God as the only God? Recite your memory verse about God found in Psalm 86:10. There are many great things about God. We learned two already—He has three different forms and He is the first and only God—but there are more! God never had to be born. He has always been alive.

IDEA WORD: God's Beginning

READ AND REMEMBER:

Genesis 1:1—"In the beginning God created the heavens and the earth."

11

THOUGHT:

If God was around to create the world in the very beginning, He could not have been created. He always was! Discuss how all people, even Jesus, are born, but not God.

HINTS:

Reread your memory verse to help your child see that God always existed, even before the world.

In Job 38:4 and Isaiah 48:13, God is reminding both men that He alone created the world. See Background Note 1 for further exposition.

After reading Hebrews 1:10–12, discuss God's eternity versus the transience of the world. See Background Note 2.

Note that His eternity stretches from the past before creation on into the future.

In Exodus 3:14, *I am* implies eternity: God always was and always will be.

DO YOU KNOW?

Since God never had to be born, no one had to create Him. He has always been alive, and He always will be alive. Therefore, we say He is *eternal*, or He will live forever.

One man wondered just how God created all the parts of the world. Read Job 38:1–30 to find out what God tells Job about His creation.

FIND OUT:

★ Read Genesis 1:1 again. In the beginning of time, before the world was created, who do we read about?

★ In the Bible, when people question God and wonder what He is doing, what does He say? Look up Job 38:4 and Isaiah 48:13.

★ Read Hebrews 1:10–12 and Psalm 102:25–27. What is the big difference between God and God's creation?

★ What does the Bible say about God's kingdom? Find the answer in Hebrews 1:8.

★ When God called Moses to lead His people out of Egypt, what did God call Himself? Turn to Exodus 3:14.

TALK TO GOD:

Thank God that He is eternal and that He will never die.

BACKGROUND NOTES:
1. As you try to comprehend the magnitude of God existing before the world, read His response to Job in Job 38:1–40:2. Through a series of rhetorical questions, God shows Job that no man can even begin to comprehend what He has done in creation. He and He alone planned and carried out His plans for the world.
2. The world created by God will someday pass away. Only God, His Word and man will live forever. This truth should compel us to invest our time and money in eternal rather than transient matters.

HANDS ON:

When you face problems this week, remember that the eternal God knows and loves you. You can tell Him your problems, and He will help you.

Memorize Genesis 1:1 — "In the beginning, God created the heavens and the earth."

How God Made Something Out of Nothing

CHILD

HINT:
How have you let God help you this week? Let your child see Him working in your life, too!

AIM:
To help your child praise and worship the God who created the world.
Note: Ethel Barrett's cassette tape and book, *Quacky and Wacky*, (Communicating Christian Values series) will help your child understand that God created us for Himself and only He can satisfy us.

THINK AGAIN:

Share how you let the eternal God help you this week. Recite your memory verse on God's beginning found in Genesis 1:1. We have learned some really amazing things about God. Not only has He always been alive, but He created the whole world out of nothing. How do we know? Because God told us in the Bible. Read on to find out how.

IDEA WORD: God's Creation

READ AND REMEMBER:

Revelation 4:11—"You are worthy, our Lord and God, to receive glory and honor and power, for you created all things, and by your will they were created and have their being."

DO YOU KNOW?

In chapter 1 of Genesis, we read how God created the whole world by only speaking the words. In six days He made and filled the earth with all kinds of living animals and trees and birds just by ordering them to come alive. To learn more about God's power to create things in the world, read Job 39.

FIND OUT:

★ How was God able to create the world? Turn to Isaiah 40:26.
★ Read Genesis 1:31. How did God feel about the world He created?
★ Who helped in the creation? The answer is in John 1:1–3 and Hebrews 1:2.
★ Read Revelation 4:11 again. What does God deserve because of His creation?
★ Turn to Ecclesiastes 12:1. What response does God want us to have to His creation?

TALK TO GOD:

Thank Jesus for creating you and the whole world for you to enjoy.

HANDS ON:

This week practice remembering that God not only created you, but everything else in

15

the world. When you look at a butterfly or a bumblebee, thank God for making these beautiful insects. For fun, think of some of the biggest things God made and some of the smallest. How many can you think of? (Hint: elephants and ants, giraffes and jellyfish, lions and ladybugs.)

Memorize Revelation 4:11—"You are worthy, our Lord and God, to receive glory and honor and power, for you created all things, and by your will they were created and have their being."

16

God's Love Is Forever

CHILD

PARENT

THINK AGAIN:

Did you remember your Creator this past week and the big and little things He created? Recite your memory verse on God's creation found in Revelation 4:11. The amazing truth of the gospel is that God, the Creator of the whole universe, cares about you and me and promises to always be with us!

IDEA WORD: God Is with Me

HINT:
Share your experience of remembering your Creator, too! Did you see anything special that made you thank God for creating the world?

READ AND REMEMBER:

Matthew 28:20b — "And surely I will be with you always, to the very end of the age."

AIM:
To help your child develop a close relationship with the Creator of the universe who cares about him.
Note: *God and Me* by Florence Heide, Concordia, 1975, is a very good book to help your child accept God's presence even when he cannot see God.

DO YOU KNOW?

THOUGHT:
Emphasize that God loves your child and wants to be with him or her always. This is a great boost to a child's self-esteem.

We have been learning that there is only one God in all the world. He never had a beginning, and He never has an ending. He is so powerful that He created the whole world! Now, for the most important

17

fact about God: He loves you and wants to be with you always.

Daniel was one person who knew that God keeps His promises about wanting to be with us always. To find out how God saved Daniel's life, read Daniel 6:1–24.

HINTS:
Discuss each of the places David mentioned in Psalm 139:7–12. See Background Note 1.

Discuss some hard times your child will face such as going to the doctor or dentist, illness, school tests, criticism, ridicule, etc. It might help to share some of your own experiences.

God promises to give us power and strength in Isaiah 40:29–31. But we must wait on the Lord in order to receive this strength. See Background Note 2.

Children have many fears. It is important to help your child see how God's presence can help him during times of fear. Psalm 56:3 is an easy memory verse to recite in times of fear.

Discuss what it means to have Jesus with us always. He can provide for all our needs and concerns. He can see and hear all we do and say, even things that are not pleasing to Him. This is a real challenge to live a holy life.

FIND OUT:

★ Where can we go to get away from God? Read Psalm 139:7–12.

★ Sometimes we go through hard times when nobody can be with us in person, but what does God promise? Turn to Isaiah 43:2.

★ Read Isaiah 40:29–31. When God is with us, what does He promise to give us?

★ When we are afraid, how should we feel? Look up Psalm 56:3.

★ As Jesus left His disciples on earth, what was His last promise? Turn again to Matthew 28:20b.

REMINDER:
Help your child pinpoint a time when he needs to know God is with him. Then quiz him or her on the memory verse. When you know of a situation that is particularly fearful for him, ask what thoughts went through his mind. Was it Matthew 28:20b?

BACKGROUND NOTES:
1. As Psalm 139:7–12 states, it is impossible to get away from God whether we climb the highest heights, descend to the lowest depths, cross the widest ocean or hide in the deepest darkness. God is still there. Paul restates this in Romans 8:38–39. Nothing can separate us from the love of God, not even death, life, angels, demons, the present, the future, any powers, height or depth, nothing!
2. "Waiting on God" does not mean closing our eyes and quickly saying, "Help me, God. Amen." Indeed, God does hear this prayer in time of crisis, but He wants us to learn to spend time with Him. This means reading His Word thoughtfully and meditatively. It means praying with our Bibles open and asking God to do for us what He has promised in His Word. It means caring more about God and what He wants than anything else in the world.

TALK TO GOD:

Thank God that He has promised to always be with you. Ask Him to help you remember that He is always with you, even when you are afraid or scared or lonely.

HANDS ON:

This week begin every day by thinking about what it means to have God always with you. Try to picture Him there. Write down some times when you really need God to be with you: when it is thundering and lightning, when a friend calls you names, when you are alone. Every time you have these feelings, recite your memory verse out loud. It will help you remember that God is always with you so there is no need to be afraid.

Memorize Matthew 28:20b—"And surely I will be with you always, to the very end of the age."

The Man Named Jesus

CHILD

THINK AGAIN:

When you were afraid, did you picture God with you? Recite your memory verse about God being with you found in Matthew 28:20b. Not only does God have a real place in our lives, but so does Jesus, His Son.

THOUGHT:
Share some of your fears as a parent: unpaid bills, hectic schedules, mounting responsibilities. How do you sense God's presence during these times? This is something you and your child should continually try to recognize and acknowledge: God's constant presence.

IDEA WORD: Jesus

AIM:
To help your child appreciate and thank Jesus for being both God and man.

READ AND REMEMBER:

John 1:1 — "In the beginning was the Word, and the Word was with God, and the Word was God."

DO YOU KNOW?

THOUGHT:
The Christmas story is familiar, but if you want to review it, see Luke 2:1–20 and Matthew 1:18–25. See Background Note 1 for a brief summary.

You probably know the Christmas story of how Jesus was born in Bethlehem in a manger nearly 2,000 years ago. But this was not the beginning of His life. Jesus has always been alive with His Father, God. It

was not until God sent Him to live on the earth that Jesus became a man. The Bible has a lot to say about Jesus being both God and man, but first read Luke 2:39–52 to learn about Jesus as a child.

HINTS:
After you read John 1:1, explain that the "Word" is Jesus.

John 1:14 is a significant verse to explain how God became man. He was God and yet He became flesh or man.

Jesus, just as any other child, grew physically and spiritually.

Although Jesus was God, He still obeyed His parents. See Background Note 2.

John 14:11 emphasizes that Jesus and God are not two gods, but one.

Help your child see that Jesus IS God. See Background Note 3.

FIND OUT:

★ Who was with God in the very beginning when He created the world? Read John 1:1 again.

★ Later on, what did this Word or Jesus do? Turn to John 1:14.

★ Read Luke 2:52. How was Jesus the same as other children in the world?

★ How did Jesus treat His parents? See Luke 2:51.

★ Look up John 14:11. What did Jesus say about God the Father?

★ Hebrews 1:3 is talking about Jesus. What does it tell us about His relationship to God?

For the Hands On assignment, help your child simply explain how Jesus was both God and man. Then help him or her decide who to share this with.

BACKGROUND NOTES:
1. The story of Jesus' birth:
a. Mary conceived a child through the Holy Spirit.
b. Joseph married her after the angel told him to.
c. Mary and Joseph went to Bethlehem to be counted according to the order of Caesar Augustus.
d. Jesus was born in a stable because all the inns were full.
2. Luke 2:51 tells us that Jesus obeyed His parents. This is important for your child to understand. Jesus was God and therefore never sinned. His earthly parents, however, were human and did make mistakes. Still, He obeyed them.
3. Hebrews 1:3 tells us that Jesus is God:
a. He is the radiance of God's glory.
b. He is the exact image of God.
c. He holds all things by His Word as does God.
4. Since God is holy, He must punish sins; but because He is merciful, He planned salvation. This salvation, however, had to be paid for by a sinless person. Only God's Son, Jesus, was sinless, so He was the only One who could die for man's sins.

TALK TO GOD:

If Jesus had not come to earth as a man, we would not know God and His love. Thank Him for this.

HANDS ON:

This week tell someone about Jesus being both God and man. After you read about Jesus as a child in the temple courts (Luke 2:39–52), you can tell your friend this story. Share why this is important to you.

Memorize John 1:1— "In the beginning was the Word, and the Word was with God, and the Word was God."

LESSON 7

An Unselfish God

CHILD

THINK AGAIN:

If you were able to tell a friend about Jesus being both God and man, how did your friend respond? Recite your memory verse on Jesus found in John 1:1. You can also share this verse with your friend. Then he or she can learn about Jesus' beginning. As both God and man, Jesus came to earth for one reason: to make a way for us to reach God.

IDEA WORD: Jesus' Life

READ AND REMEMBER:

John 6:38 — "For I have come down from heaven not to do my will but to do the will of him who sent me."

DO YOU KNOW?

Jesus lived on the earth for 33 years, and we can read in the Bible about many of His miracles and of the stories He told. But the Bible tells us there was one

reason why Jesus came to earth. Read John 4:1–26 to see how Jesus came to point people to God.

HINTS:
Discuss the difference between condemnation and salvation. See the Background Note for the distinction.

After reading your memory verse, discuss what God's will was: to provide eternal life for man.

There is only one way to come to God according to John 14:6 and that is through Jesus Christ.

Jesus told people that His purpose on earth was "to give His life as a ransom for many" (Matthew 20:28).

Jesus promises not only to give us life, but the very best life possible.

After examining Jesus' life, it is our responsibility to believe. See also John 20:31 where John states that the whole purpose of his book is so that people might believe Jesus.

FIND OUT:

★ In John 3:17, what was *not* God's reason for sending Jesus? What *was* His reason?

★ Read your memory verse. What did Jesus say He *did not* come to do? What *did* He come to do?

★ Can we know God without knowing Jesus? Turn to John 14:6.

★ Why did Jesus come to earth? Read Matthew 20:28.

★ What does Jesus want to give us? Look up John 10:10b.

★ As we look at Jesus' life and all that He did on earth, what should we do? The answer is in John 14:11.

REMINDER:
Do you desire to live your life in obedience to God?

BACKGROUND NOTE:
God did not send Jesus to condemn people but to save them. If Jesus had come to condemn us, He would have told everyone all the wrong things they did; He would have let the sick suffer and die; He would have exultantly proclaimed hell as man's destiny. But this was not Jesus' reason for coming. He came to save people. He was anxious to show them a better way of life. And He offered Himself as the only means to that life. He even promised eternal life beginning now and continuing in heaven.

TALK TO GOD:

Jesus spent His whole life obeying His Father instead of doing the things He wanted to do. Thank Him for obeying God and being unselfish. Ask Him to help you spend your life obeying God, too. Some ways you can obey God are obeying your parents, being nice to people or helping a person in need.

HANDS ON:

Begin each day thinking about your memory verse. Ask Jesus to help you obey God's will that day.

Memorize John 6:38—"For I have come down from heaven not to do my will but to do the will of him who sent me."

25

LESSON 8

God's Bridge to Us

CHILD

THINK AGAIN:

Share how God helped you do His will this week. Recite your memory verse on Jesus' life found in John 6:38. Jesus spent His life doing God's will. He wanted to heal people from their sicknesses and teach them about God's love. But He still had to carry out God's reason for sending Him to earth and that was to die on a cross for man's sins and rise again.

IDEA WORD: Jesus' Death and Rising Again

READ AND REMEMBER:

1 Corinthians 15:3–4 — "For what I received I passed on to you as of first importance: that Christ died for our sins according to the Scriptures, that he was buried, that he was raised on the third day according to the Scriptures."

DO YOU KNOW?

As we have seen, Jesus spent His whole life doing God's will. It was not always easy for Him to do

26

what God had planned, but He knew it was what God wanted Him to do. Jesus even knew that He was going to die on a cross and that it would be a very painful, slow death, but He still wanted to obey God. We can be glad that Jesus did obey God, because three days after He died, He arose from the dead and conquered sin and death for us! You can read about Jesus' death on the cross in John 19:16–37.

HINTS:
Be sure your child realizes that only Jesus can be our mediator with God because He was sinless.

Jesus predicts His death in John 16:16 though the disciples did not understand it. See also Matthew 16:21–22.

Note the three points Paul mentions in 1 Corinthians 15:3–4: Jesus' death, burial and resurrection.

In 1 Peter 3:18, note that Jesus, being righteous, had never sinned, but He had to suffer for the sins of the unrighteous — us.

Note our condition at the time of Jesus' death: we were still sinners.

FIND OUT:

★ God is holy and man is sinful. How can they be brought together? Find 1 Timothy 2:5–6.

★ As Jesus ate His last supper with His disciples, what did He tell them would happen? Read John 16:16.

★ Read 1 Corinthians 15:3–4 again. When Paul preached, what did he tell the people?

★ Turn to 1 Peter 3:18. Was Jesus suffering for any sin of His own or for our sins?

★ Did we deserve to have Jesus die for us? The answer is in Romans 5:8.

TALK TO GOD:

Thank Jesus for obeying God and dying on the cross for our sins when we did not deserve it.

HANDS ON:

On construction paper, draw or trace a large bridge. At one end write GOD and at the other end write ME. Spaced across the bridge write J E S U S. This will help you remember that the only way to get to God is to cross over with Jesus.

Memorize 1 Corinthians 15:3–4 — "For what I received I passed on to you as of first importance: that Christ died for our sins according to the Scriptures, that he was buried, that he was raised on the third day according to the Scriptures."

Jesus Is Coming Back

PARENT

CHILD

THINK AGAIN:

Can you remember who is the only bridge to God? Recite your memory verse on Jesus' death and resurrection found in 1 Corinthians 15:3–4. After Jesus died on the cross and rose from the dead, He returned to heaven, but the Bible tells us that some day He will come back for us!

IDEA WORD: Jesus Returns

READ AND REMEMBER:

Matthew 24:44 — "So you also must be ready, because the Son of Man will come at an hour when you do not expect him."

AIM:
To help your child prepare for Christ's return by living a holy life.

THOUGHT:
Christians have been expecting Christ to return for 2,000 years. Though He has not come back yet, we must expect Him at any time.

DO YOU KNOW?

After living on earth for 33 years, Jesus returned to heaven. But He promised His disciples that He would come back to get them and everyone else who

believes in Him. He even told a story to show us how we should live while we wait for Him. You can read it in Matthew 25:1–13.

HINTS:
Read Acts 1:6–11 for background on Jesus' return. Discuss the manner of Jesus' return to earth. See Background Note 1 for help.

No one knows precisely when Jesus is coming back, neither the angels nor Jesus Himself. Only God the Father knows the appointed time.

The purpose of Jesus' return is to take believers to their prepared home in heaven.

As you discuss Jesus' return, remind your child that as Christians we will be with God forever. See Background Note 2 for an outline of 1 Thessalonians 4:16–17.

Emphasize the need for holiness as we wait for Jesus to come back. Read Background Note 3.

FIND OUT:

★ When Jesus went up to heaven in the clouds, the disciples kept watching until two angels came. What did the angels promise? Read Acts 1:11 for the answer.

★ Read Matthew 24:36. Who knows when Jesus is coming back?

★ Why is Jesus coming back? Look up John 14:3.

★ What will happen when Jesus does come back? Read 1 Thessalonians 4:16–17.

★ What should we do as we wait for Jesus to come again? Find the answer in Matthew 24:42–44.

BACKGROUND NOTES:
1. Jesus was taken up to heaven from the Mount of Olives. As the disciples watched Him go, He disappeared into a cloud. When the angels came to address the disciples, they announced that Jesus would come back to earth just as He had left it—through the clouds in the sky.
2. First Thessalonians 4:16–17 describes what will happen when Jesus comes back to earth:
a. He will come with a shout, the voice of the archangel and the trumpet of God.
b. The bodies of those who have already died in Christ will be resurrected to join their spirits which are in heaven.
c. Those who are alive will be caught up in the clouds to meet the Lord. (Note that 1 Corinthians 15:52 says this will all happen in just a twinkling of an eye.)
3. Since we do not know when Christ will return, believers are to always be ready. The illustration is given of a thief breaking into a house. If the owner had known when the thief was coming, he would have been ready. We, too, do not know when Jesus is coming again, but we must be ready at any time. First John 3:2–3 also challenges us to live a life of purity as we anticipate Christ's return.

TALK TO GOD:

Thank Jesus for promising to come back and take us to heaven. Since Jesus can come back at any time, ask Him to help you live a holy life so you will always be ready to meet Him.

HANDS ON:

This week begin every day by remembering that Jesus is coming back soon—maybe today! Ask your mother or father to help you make a list of things you can do to live a holy life. At the top of your list write "Ways to Be Ready to Meet Jesus." Your list might include these examples: (1) Obey my parents, (2) Look for nice things to do for people, (3) Don't start fights, (4) Learn more about Jesus by going to Sunday school and church.

Memorize Matthew 24:44—"So you also must be ready, because the Son of Man will come at an hour when you do not expect him."

A Special Helper from God

CHILD

THINK AGAIN:

Did you start your list of "Ways to Be Ready to Meet Jesus?" Read some of the things you need to do before Jesus comes. If you need help, ask your parents again. Recite your memory verse about Jesus coming back found in Matthew 24:44. Jesus does not live on earth today, but God has sent the Holy Spirit to live with us and in us. This special helper from God will help you be just what God wants you to be.

IDEA WORD: Holy Spirit's Work

READ AND REMEMBER:

"But the Counselor, the Holy Spirit, whom the Father will send in my name, will teach you all things and will remind you of everything I have said to you."

DO YOU KNOW?

When Jesus left His disciples to go back to heaven, He did not leave them alone. Instead He sent them another Person of the Trinity, the Holy Spirit. While Jesus lived on earth, He could only be in one place at one time, but the Holy Spirit can be everywhere at once. You can read about the very first day the Holy Spirit came to live in Christians in Acts 2:1–13.

FIND OUT:

★ Read John 14:26 again. Who is sending the Holy Spirit? What is another name for the Holy Spirit? What two jobs will the Holy Spirit have?

★ Read John 16:13–14. What is one more name for the Holy Spirit? What will the Holy Spirit do?

★ There are some things that people do not know about God. How does God show these things to us? Find the answer in 1 Corinthians 2:9–10.

★ When we tell people about Jesus, it is not our words that make them believe in Him. What does make them believe? The answer is in 1 Corinthians 2:4–5.

TALK TO GOD:

Thank Jesus for sending His Holy Spirit to help you live as a Christian.

THOUGHT:
For your own background on the promise of the Holy Spirit, read John 14–17 on Jesus' final instructions to His disciples and His prayer to the Father before His death. Help your child see how tremendous it is to have the Holy Spirit with him or her all the time.

HINTS:
In John 14:26, you will read that the Holy Spirit has come from the Father. (See also John 14:16.) Discuss the two jobs of the Holy Spirit: teaching all things that we need to know and reminding us of all Jesus said.

Note the jobs of this "Spirit of Truth" found in John 16:13–14. See the Background Note for detail.

The Holy Spirit brings conviction of sin. When we feel guilty after we do something wrong, it is because the Holy Spirit has convicted us.

God reveals certain mysteries to us through His Spirit so that we may have a glimpse of what "God has prepared for those who love Him" (1 Corinthians 2:9–10).

Our task in witnessing is important; but it is the Spirit who convicts.

Help your child realize that the Holy Spirit is here to meet every need he or she has.

Help your child decide what work of the Holy Spirit he needs the most right now. Refer back to the Find Out section for specific jobs of the Holy Spirit.

BACKGROUND NOTE:

The jobs of the Spirit of Truth are found in John 16:13–14.
1. He guides into truth.
2. He speaks from God, not His own ideas.
3. He tells what will happen.
4. He brings glory and honor to Jesus.

HANDS ON:

This week think about the work the Holy Spirit wants to do for you. He wants to help you remember what Jesus said in the Bible, and He wants to tell you when you are upsetting God by deciding to do bad things. Pick out an area where you need special help and ask the Holy Spirit to help you.

Memorize John 14:26 — "But the Counselor, the Holy Spirit, whom the Father will send in my name, will teach you all things and will remind you of everything I have said to you."

The Helper's Home

CHILD

THINK AGAIN:

How did the Holy Spirit help you last week? Recite your memory verse on the Holy Spirit's work found in John 14:26. The Holy Spirit not only wants to teach you, help you and remind you, but He also wants to live *in* you.

IDEA WORD: Holy Spirit in Me

READ AND REMEMBER:

Galatians 5:16 — "So I say, live by the Spirit, and you will not gratify the desires of the sinful nature."

DO YOU KNOW?

The Holy Spirit did not come to the world to live in trees or stones or animals. He needs a special home — the hearts of boys and girls and mothers and dads. But He will not live in just any heart. The Holy Spirit's home must be the pure heart of a boy or girl wanting to live for Jesus. The Holy Spirit wants to live in you and help you. Read John 14:15–31 to find out how the Holy Spirit wants to help Christians. Does the Holy Spirit live in you?

FIND OUT:

- ★ Read Galatians 4:6. Who are the only ones who will receive God's Holy Spirit?
- ★ How can a Christian keep from doing the bad things that he or she is tempted to do? Read Galatians 5:16 again.
- ★ When a Christian has God's Spirit in him, how is he different? The answer is in Romans 8:9.

TALK TO GOD:

Thank Jesus for sending His Holy Spirit to live in your heart all the time. Ask Him to help you be filled with this Spirit so you will not want to do bad things.

HANDS ON:

When you feel confused about whether to do something good or bad, remember that *you* can decide to follow God's way. The Holy Spirit will show you what is right and what is wrong.

Memorize Galatians 5:16 — "So I say, live by the Spirit, and you will not gratify the desires of the sinful nature."

HINTS:
After reading Galatians 4:6, emphasize that the Holy Spirit will only live in the believer.

Explain that substituting alcohol, drugs, money or anything in place of God's love is sin. Instead, we should fill our bodies with the Holy Spirit.

The challenge in Galatians 5:16 is to let the Holy Spirit tell you how to live. When this happens, the believer no longer does what he is tempted to do.

When the Holy Spirit lives in you, a believer does not have to live for and obey the flesh. See the Background Note.

BACKGROUND NOTE:
Romans 8:9 tells how a believer with God's Spirit lives. No longer is he controlled by the sinful nature. This nature will still try to tell him how to live. But if a person belongs to Christ, he has the Spirit of Christ living in him. It is this new Spirit that now wants to control the believer.